The Coloring Book Belongs to:

_____

Copyright 2020 Clint Atelier Books
Auther&Artest: Clint Smith
ClintAtelier.com

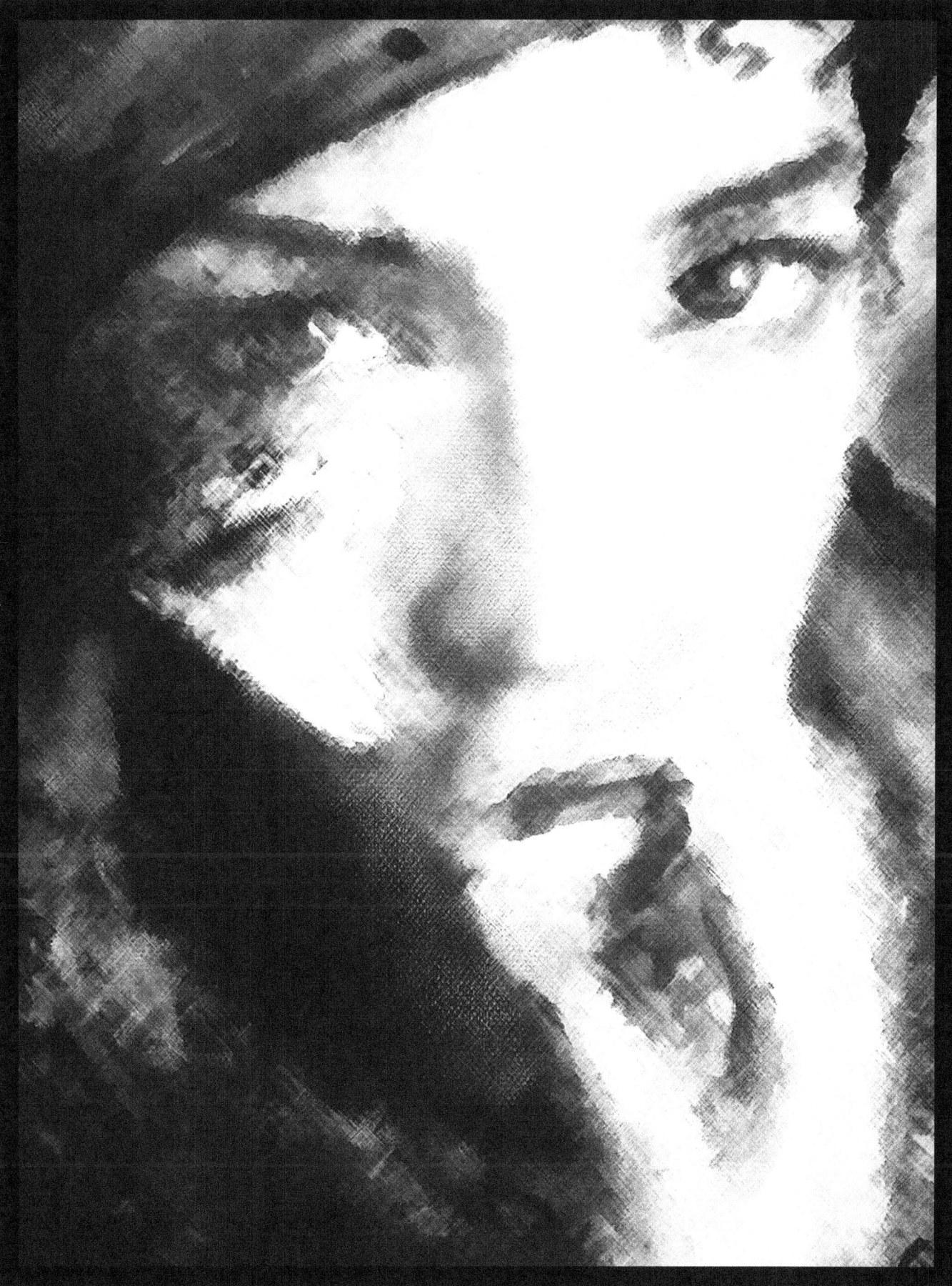

Copyright 2020 Clint Atelier Books
Auther&Artest: Clint Smith
ClintAtelier.com

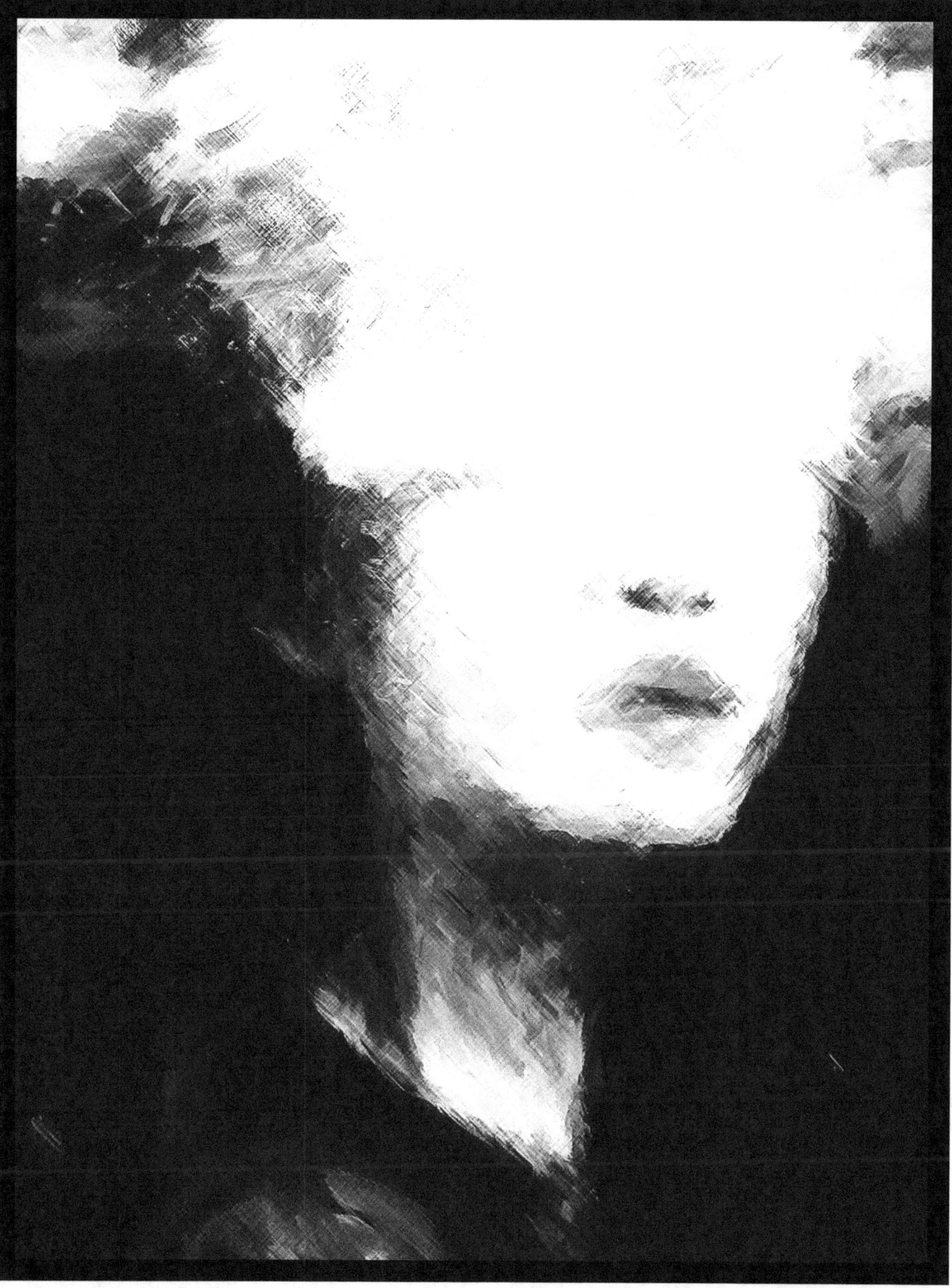

Copyright 2020 Clint Atelier Books
Auther&Artest: Clint Smith
ClintAtelier.com

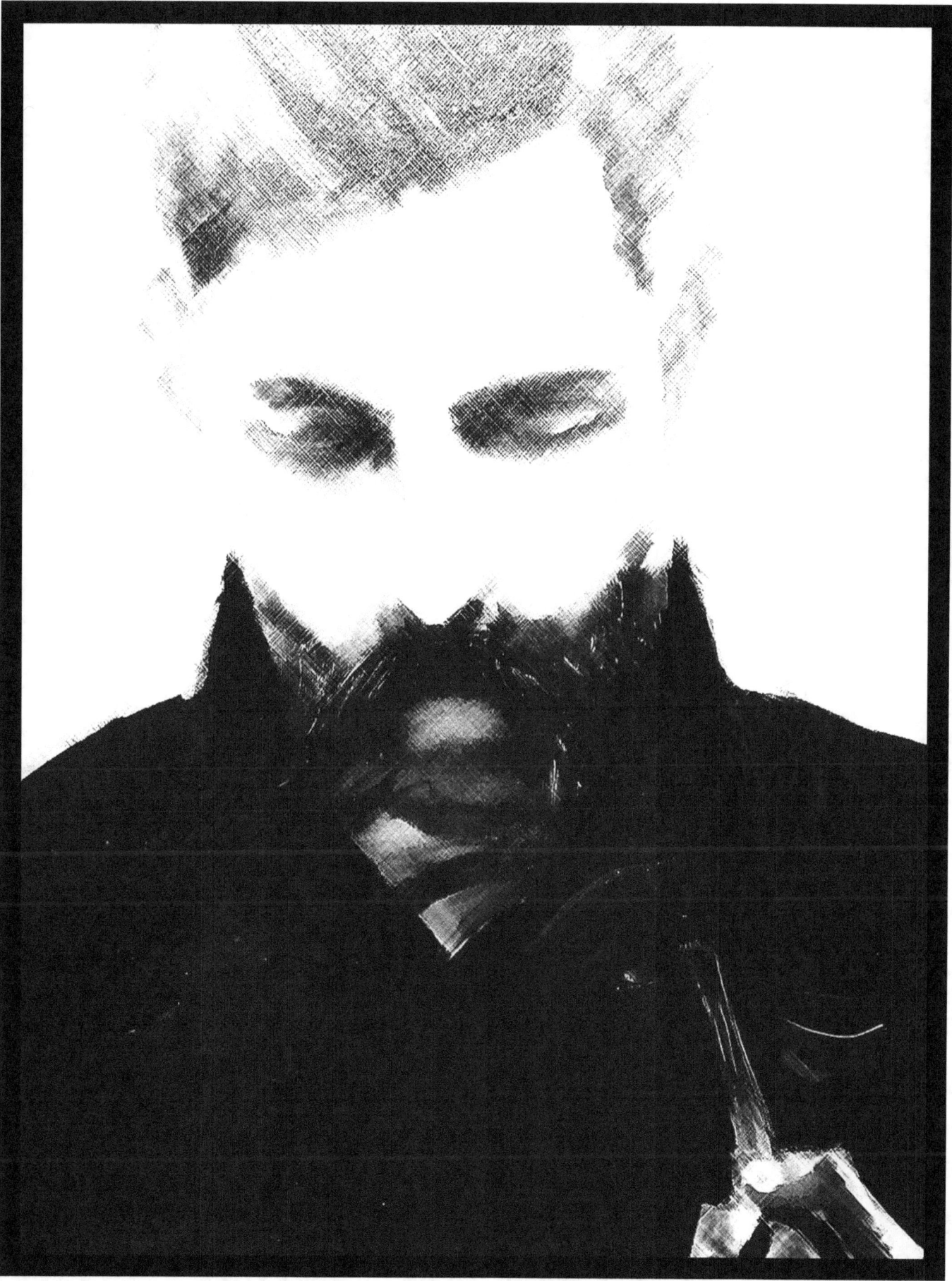

Copyright 2020 Clint Atelier Books
Auther&Artest: Clint Smith
ClintAtelier.com

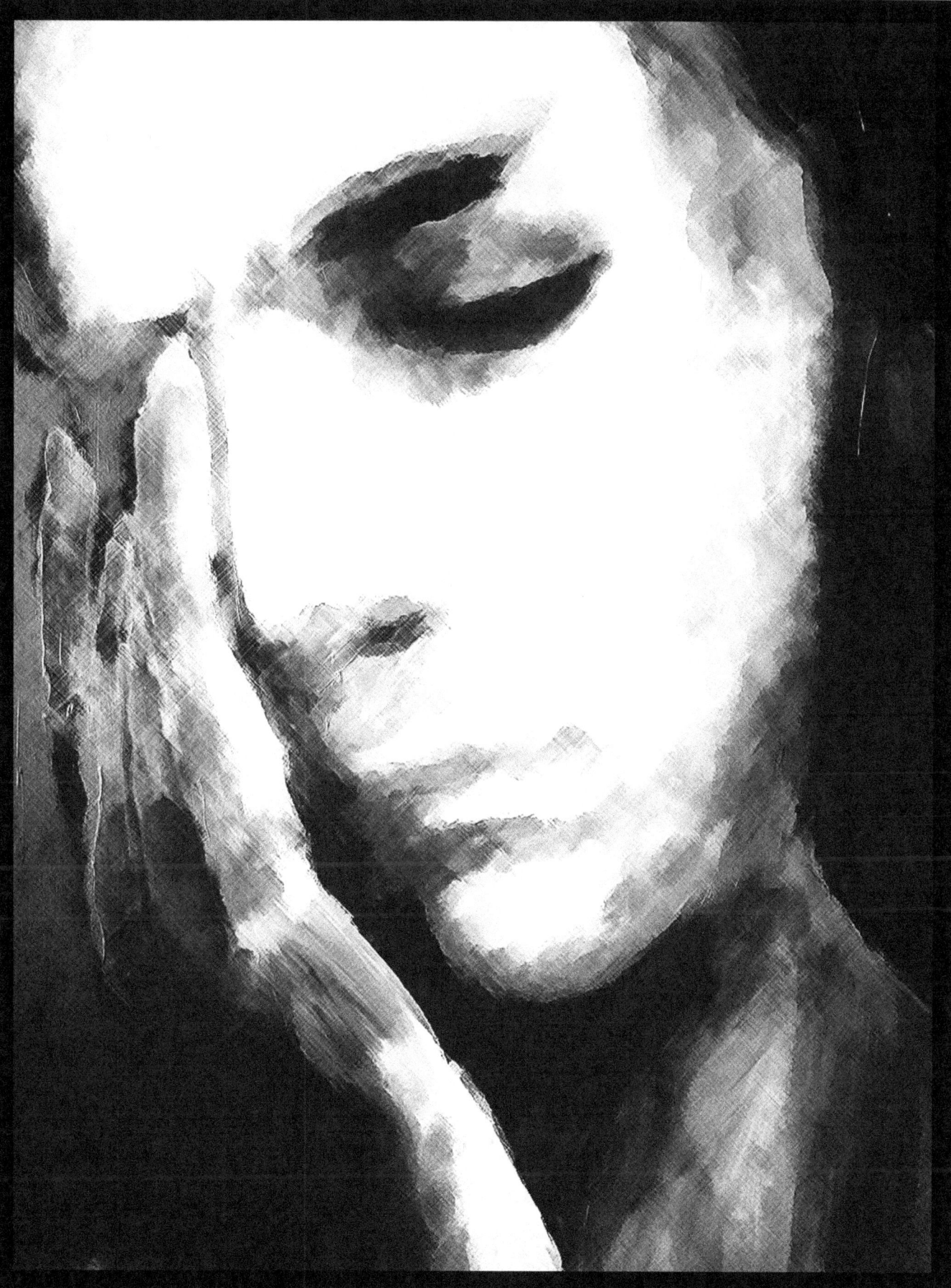

Copyright 2020 Clint Atelier Books
Auther&Artest: Clint Smith
ClintAtelier.com

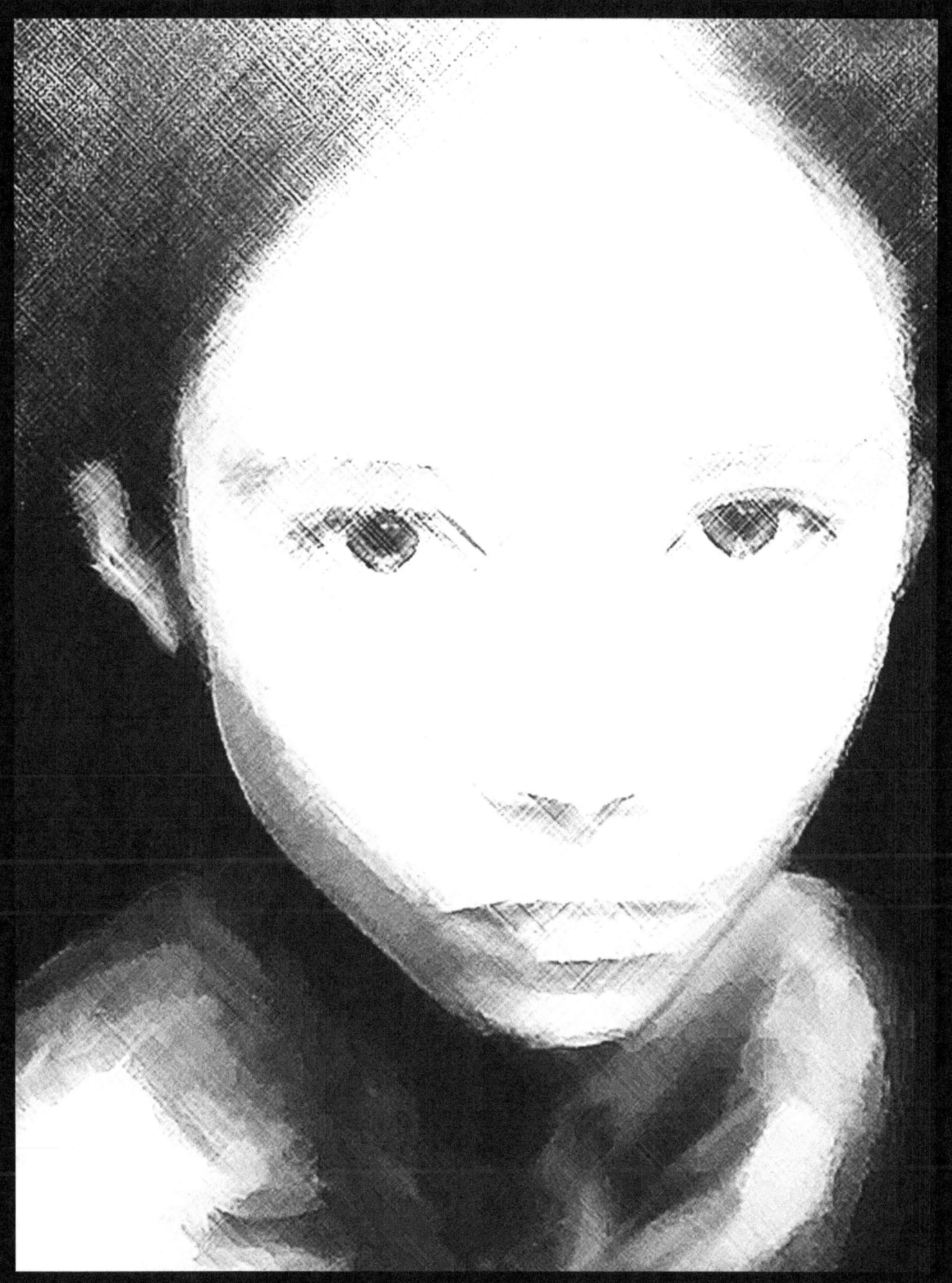

Copyright 2020 Clint Atelier Books
Auther&Artest: Clint Smith
ClintAtelier.com

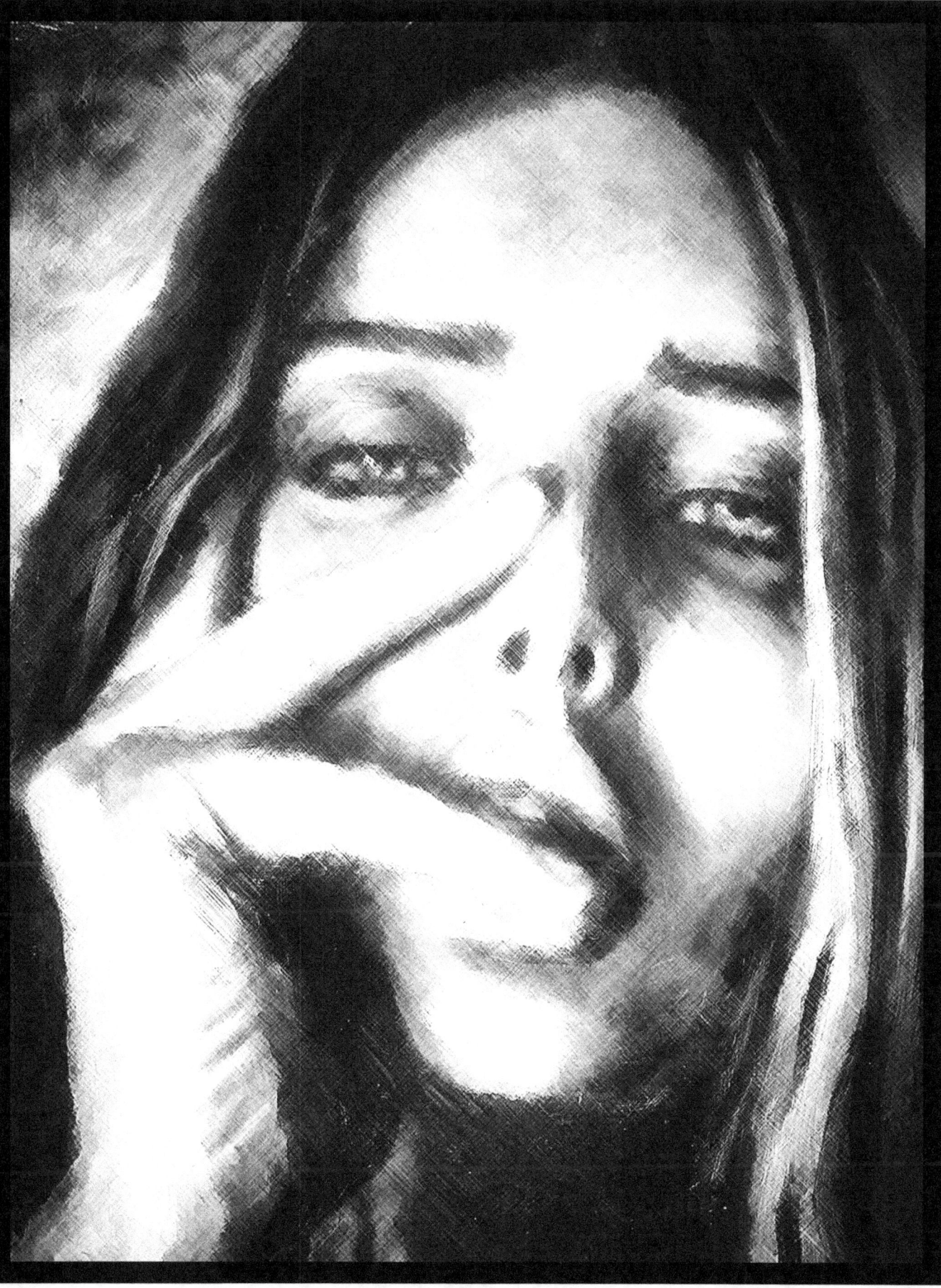

Copyright 2020 Clint Atelier Books
Auther&Artest: Clint Smith
ClintAtelier.com

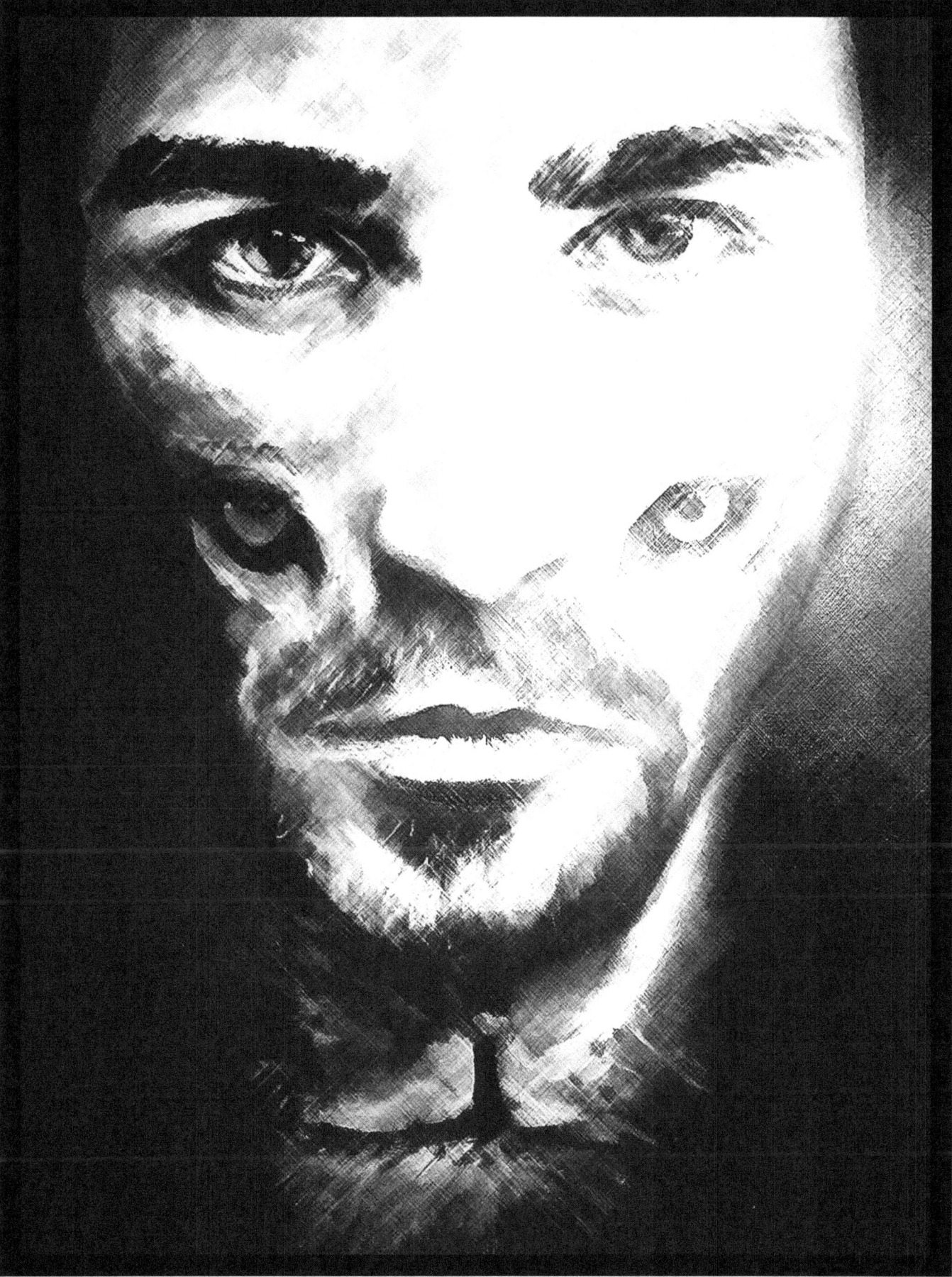

Copyright 2020 Clint Atelier Books
Auther&Artest: Clint Smith
ClintAtelier.com

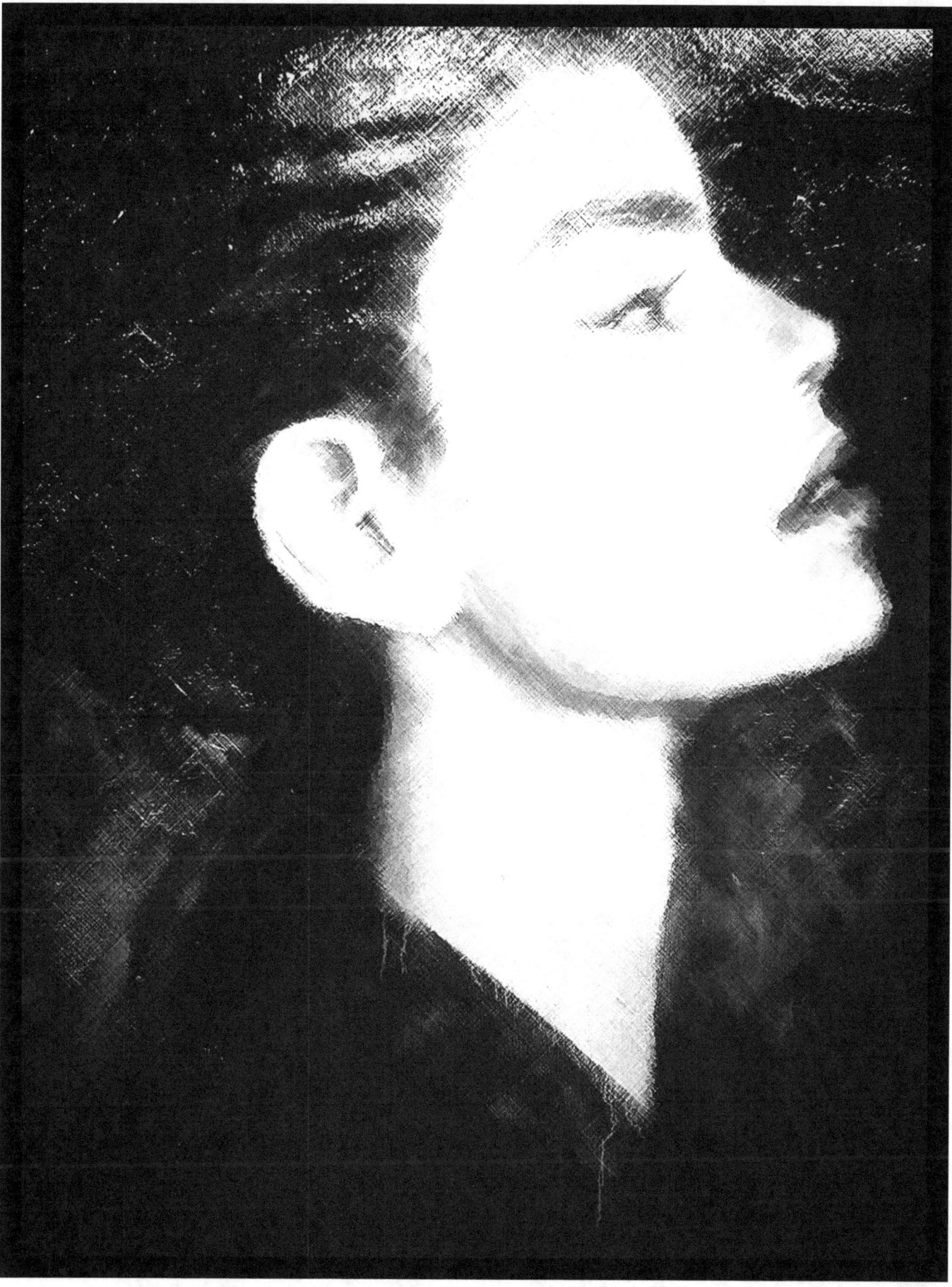

Copyright 2020 Clint Atelier Books
Auther&Artest: Clint Smith
ClintAtelier.com

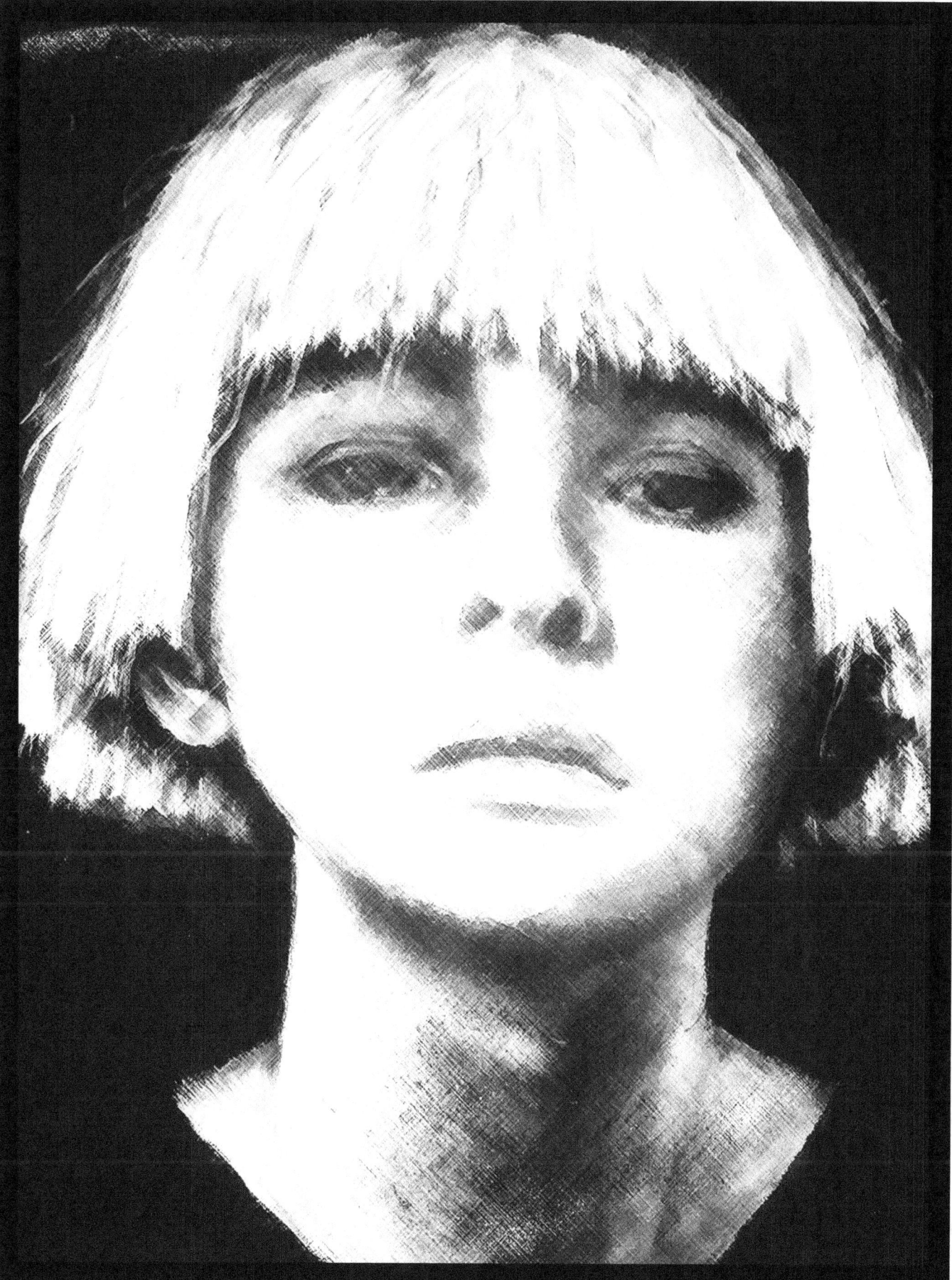

Copyright 2020 Clint Atelier Books
Auther&Artest: Clint Smith
ClintAtelier.com

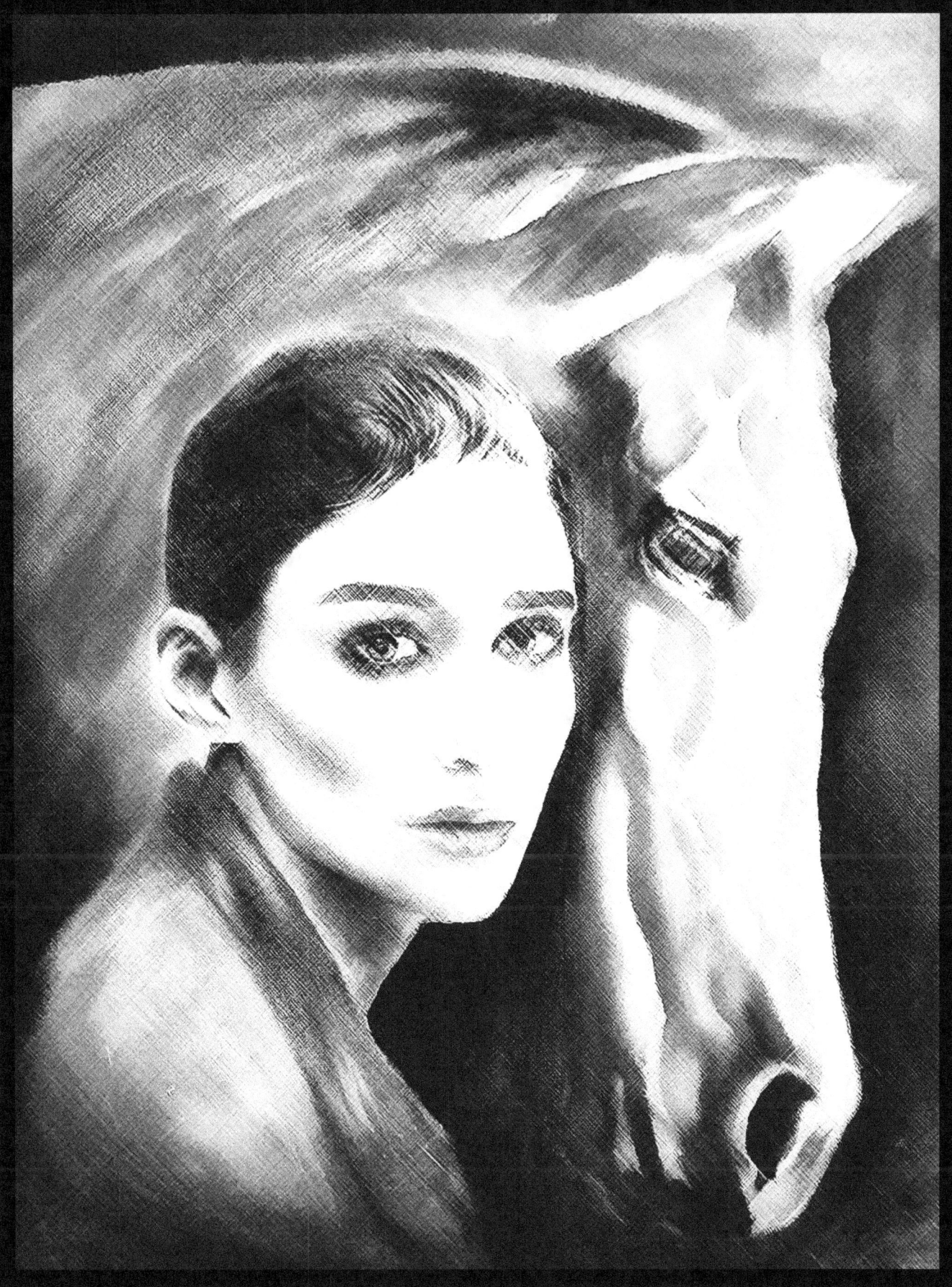

Copyright 2020 Clint Atelier Books
Auther&Artest: Clint Smith
ClintAtelier.com

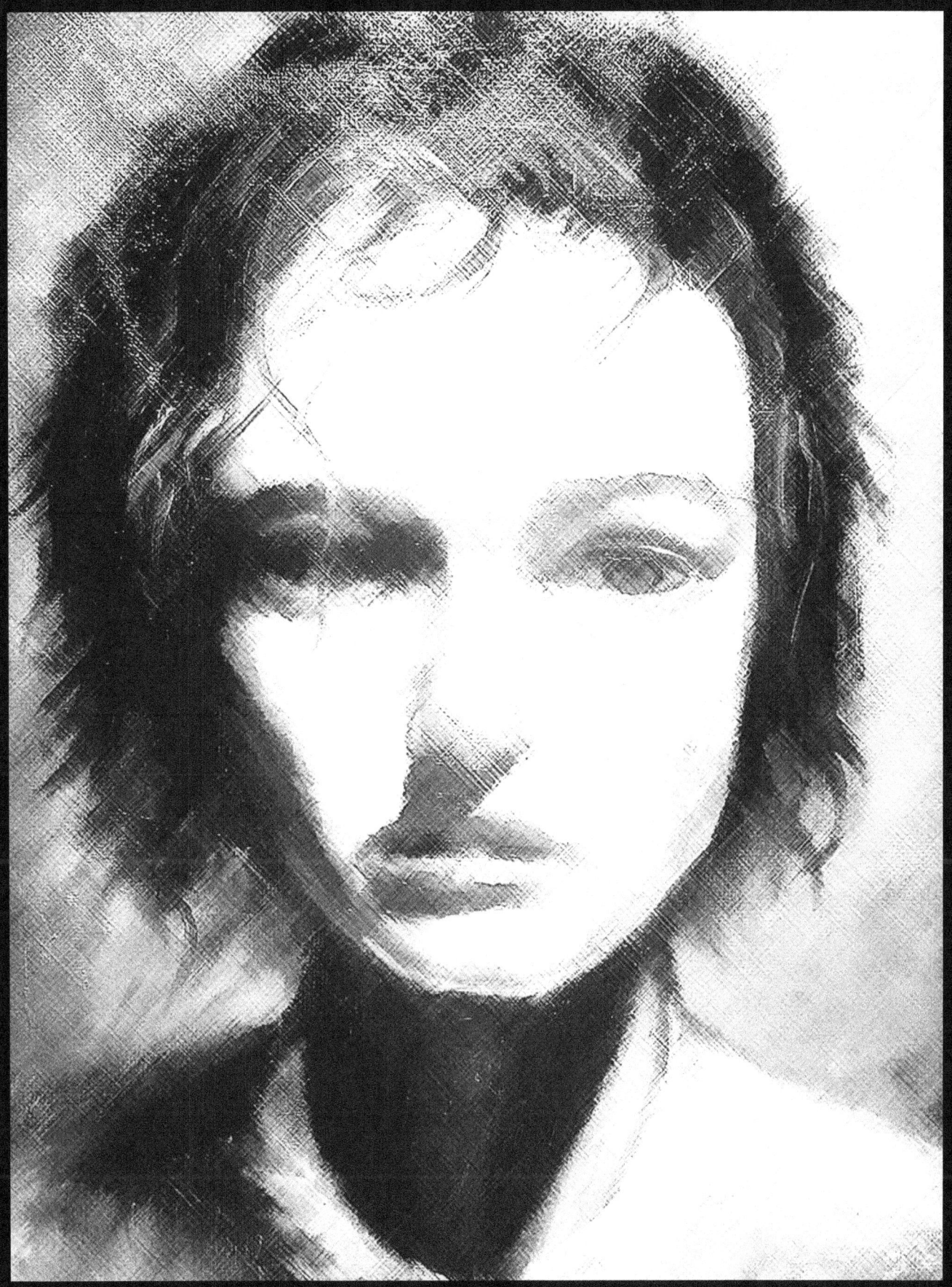

Copyright 2020 Clint Atelier Books
Auther&Artest: Clint Smith
ClintAtelier.com

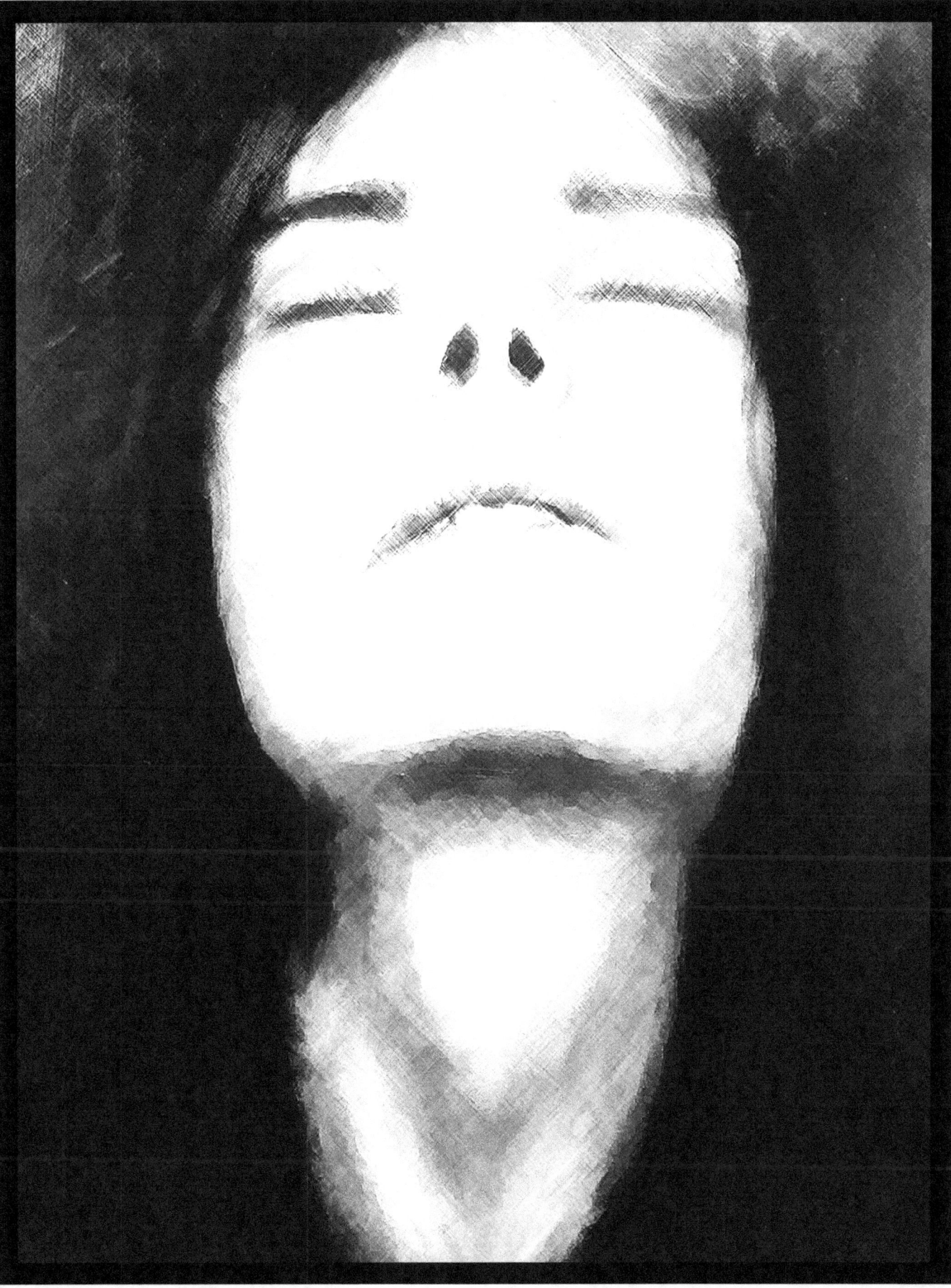

Copyright 2020 Clint Atelier Books
Auther&Artest: Clint Smith
ClintAtelier.com

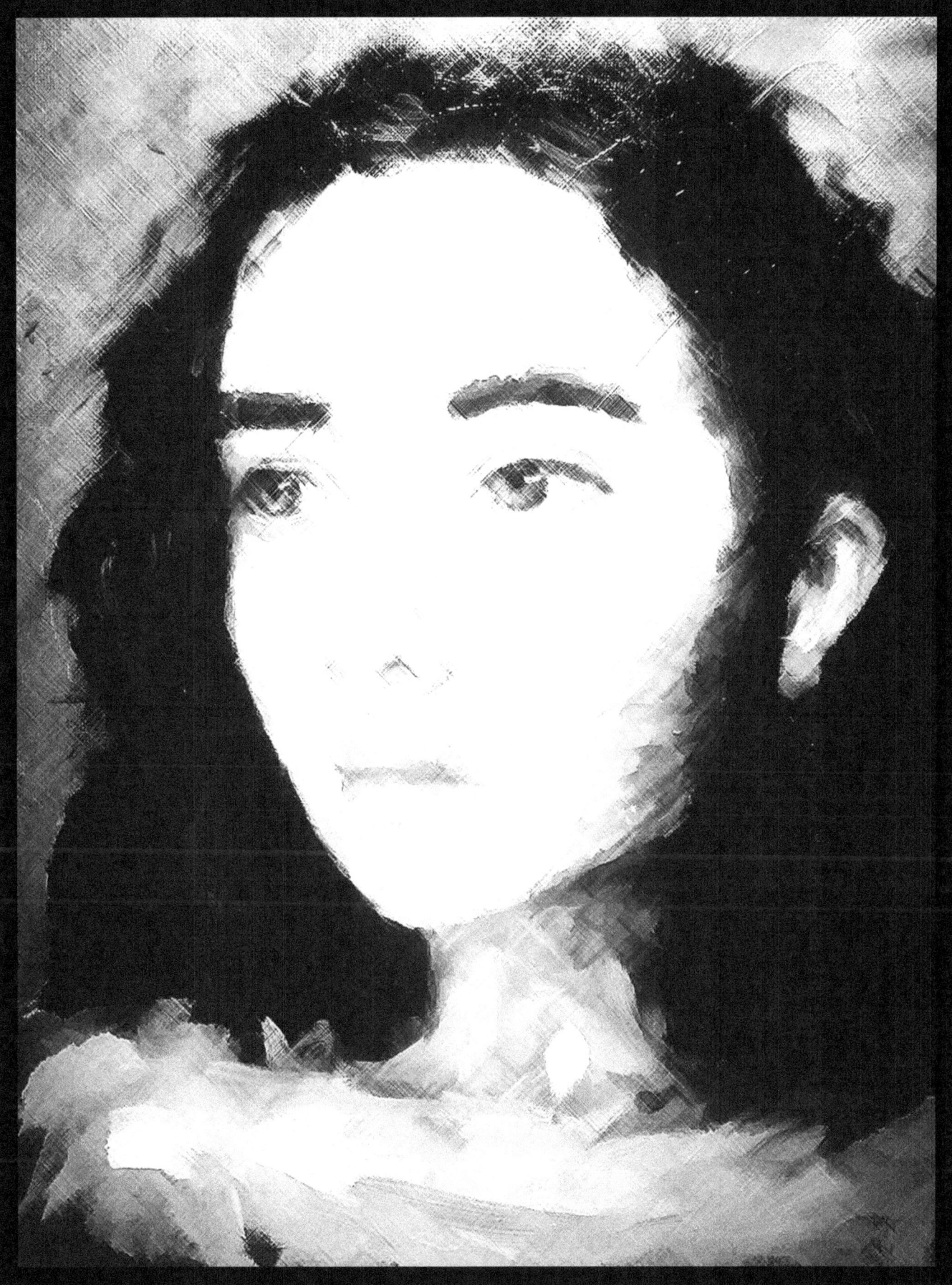

Copyright 2020 Clint Atelier Books
Auther&Artest: Clint Smith
ClintAtelier.com

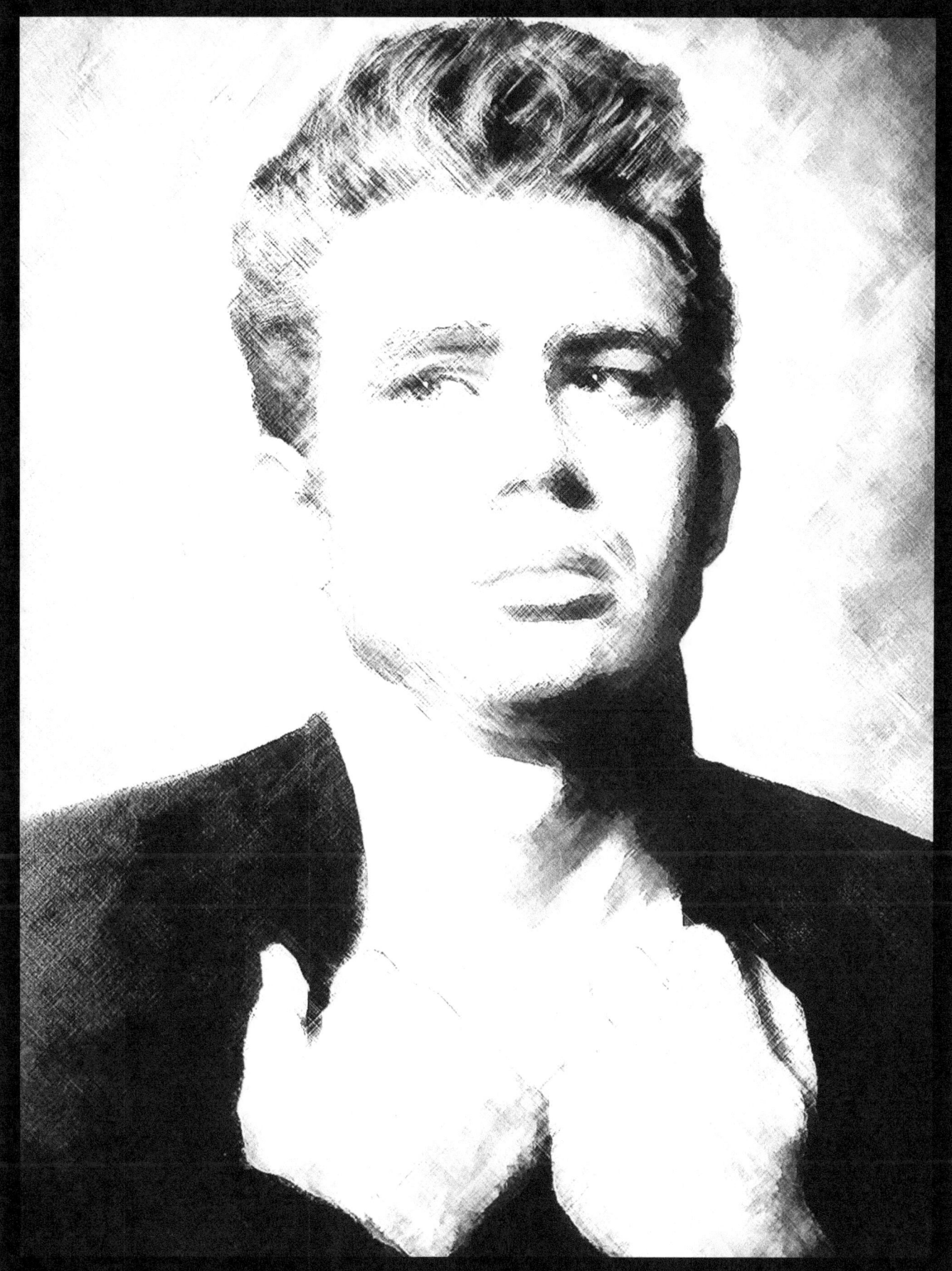

Copyright 2020 Clint Atelier Books
Auther&Artest: Clint Smith
ClintAtelier.com

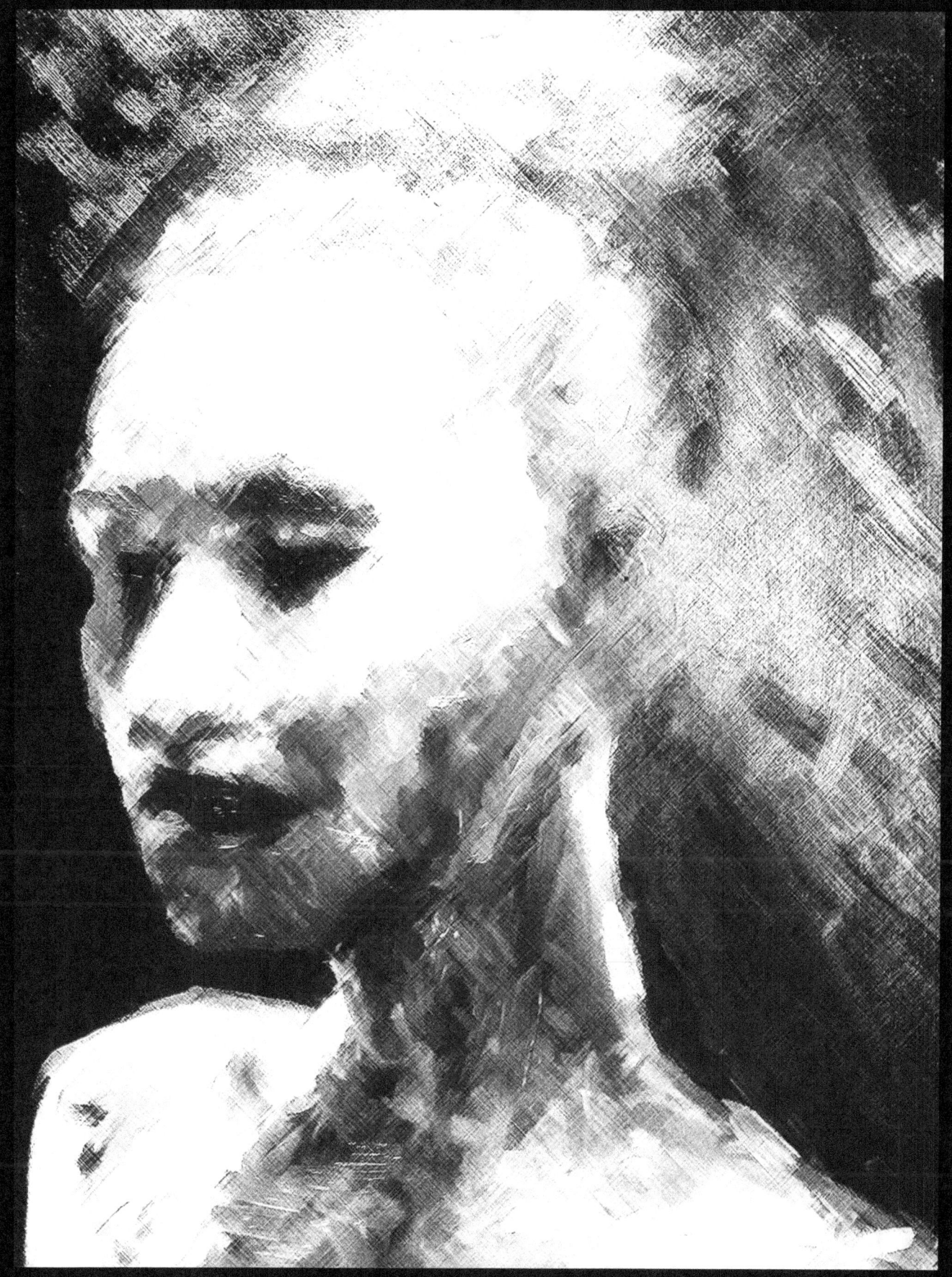

Copyright 2020 Clint Atelier Books
Auther&Artest: Clint Smith
ClintAtelier.com

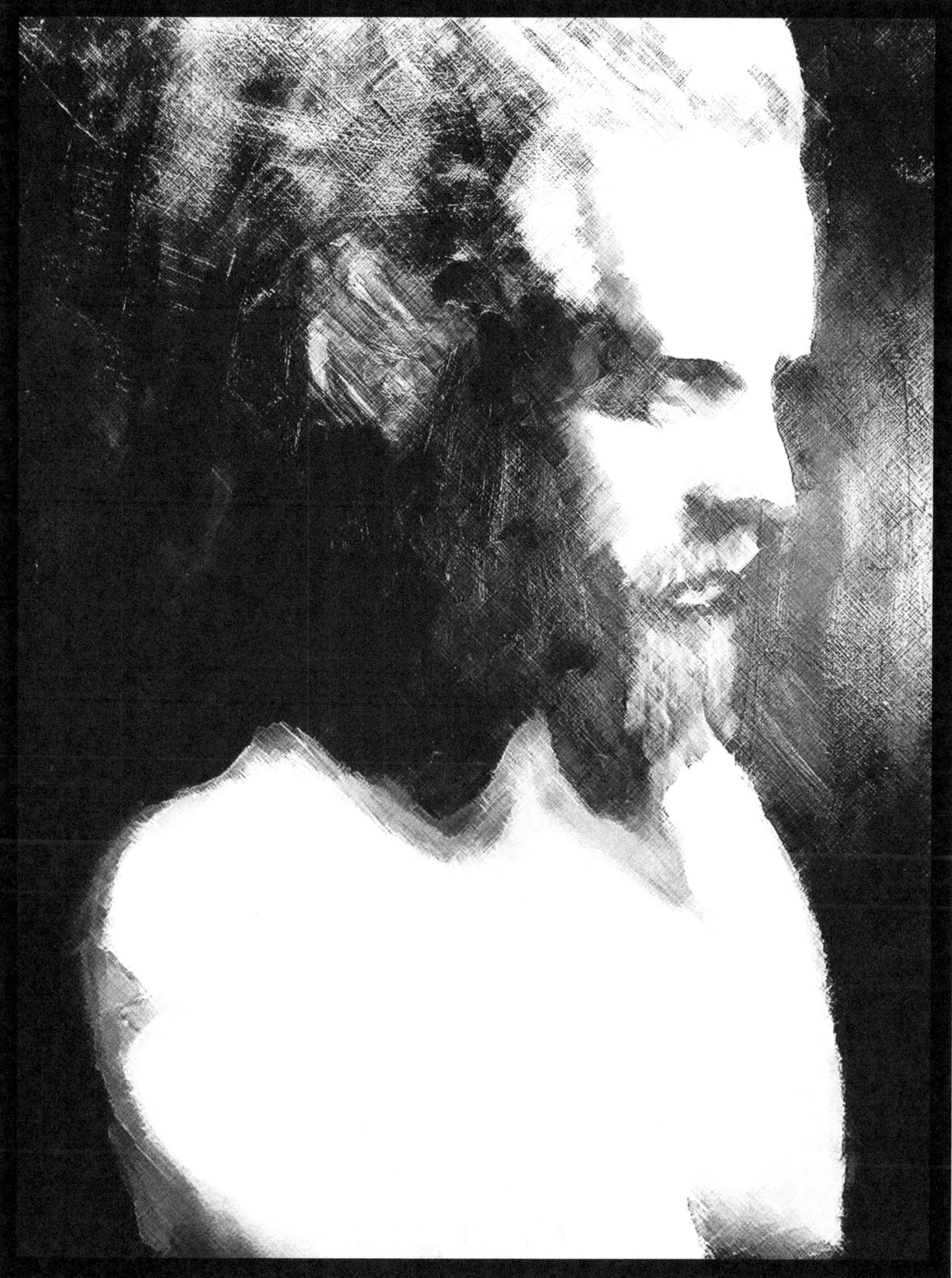

Copyright 2020 Clint Atelier Books
Auther&Artest: Clint Smith
ClintAtelier.com

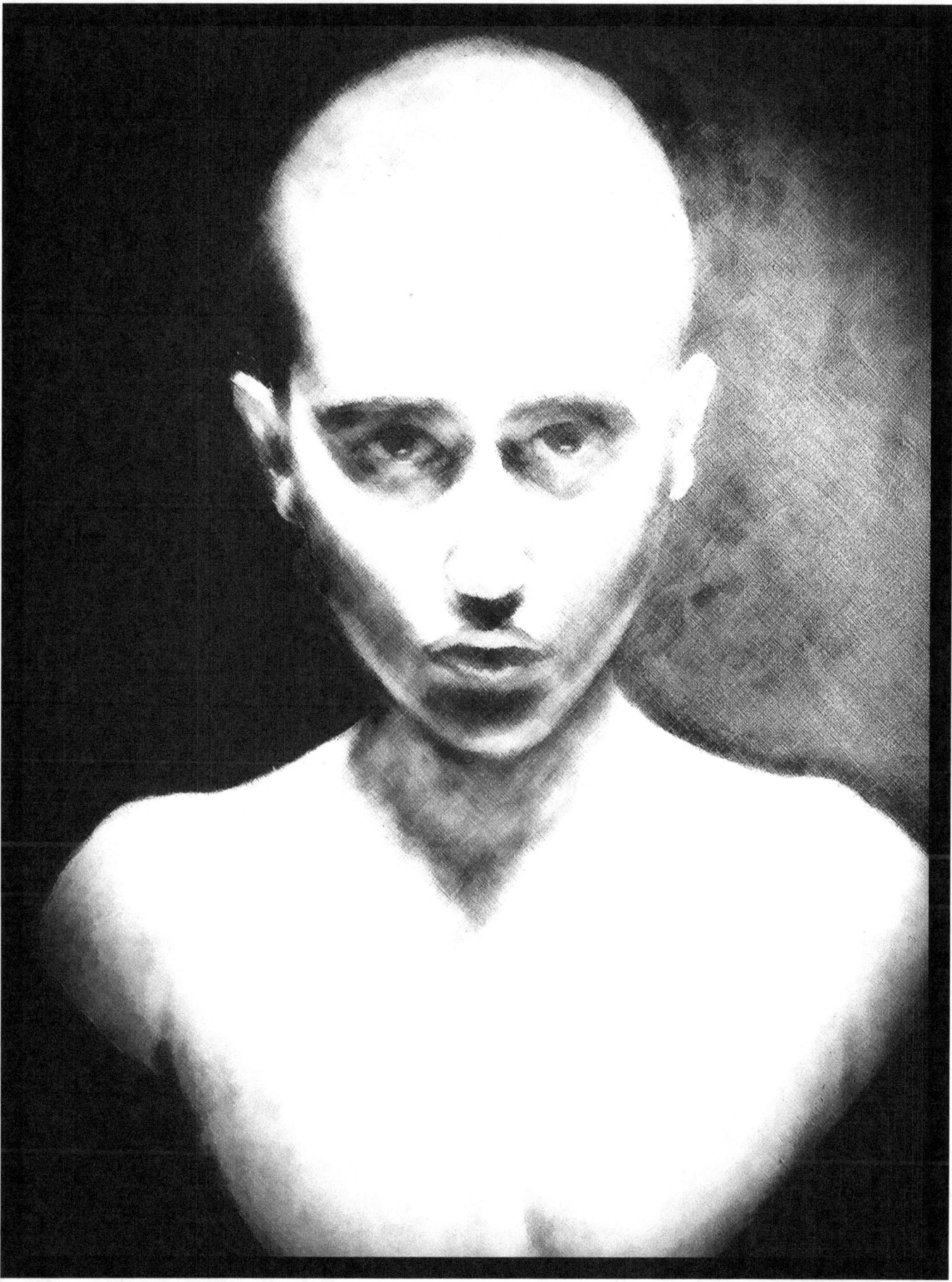

Copyright 2020 Clint Atelier Books
Auther&Artest: Clint Smith
ClintAtelier.com

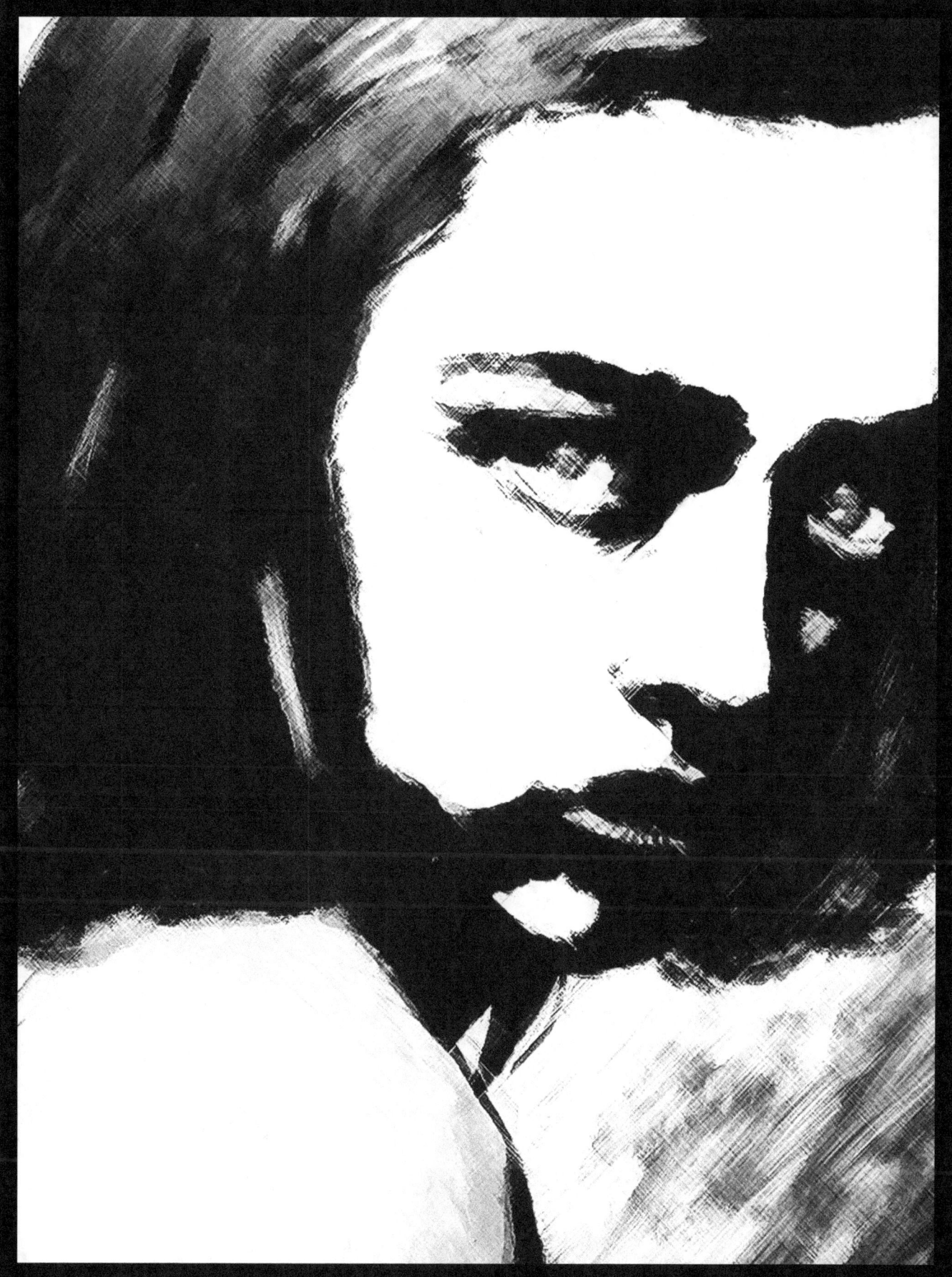

Copyright 2020 Clint Atelier Books
Auther&Artest: Clint Smith
ClintAtelier.com

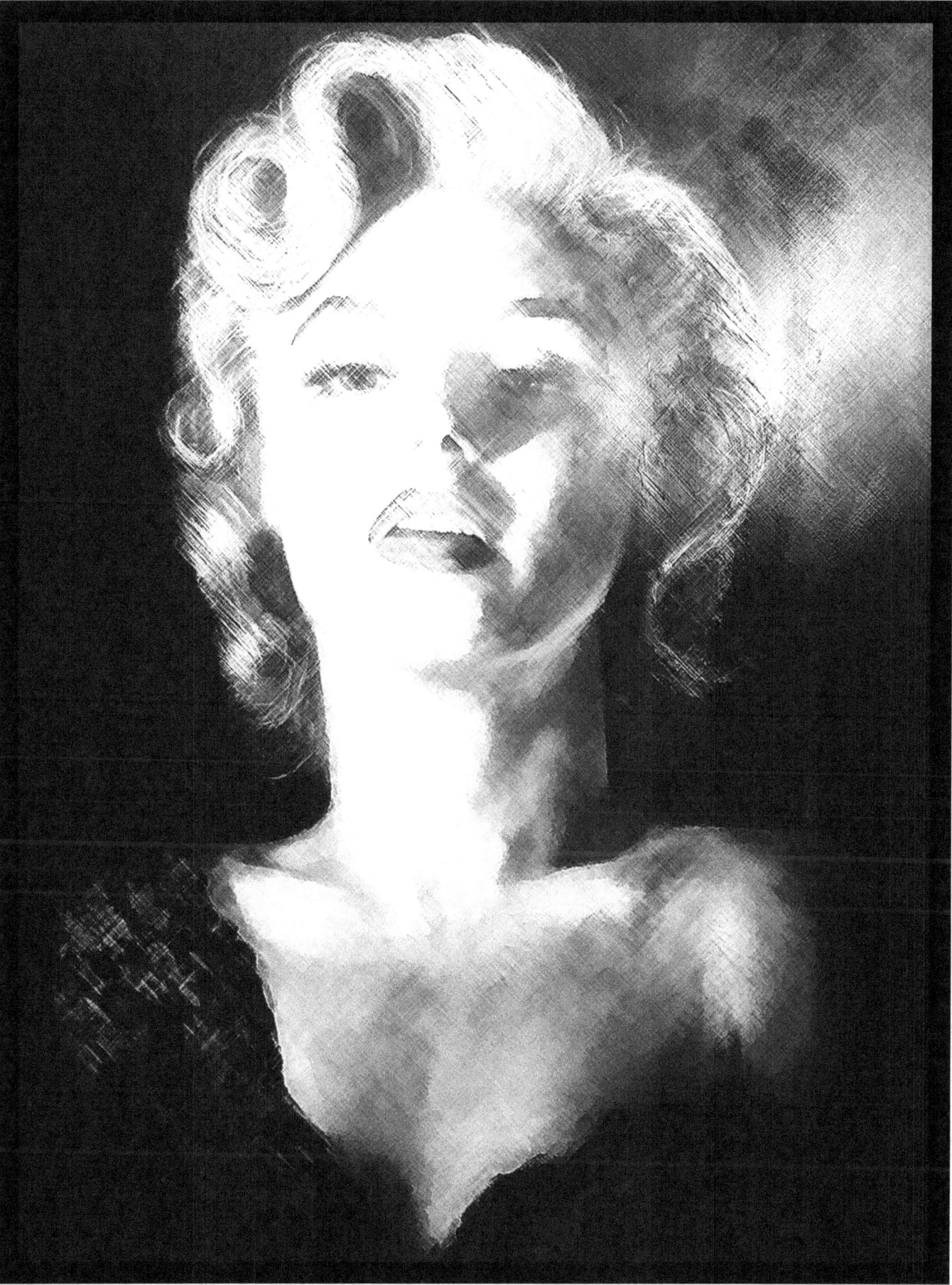

Copyright 2020 Clint Atelier Books
Auther&Artest: Clint Smith
ClintAtelier.com

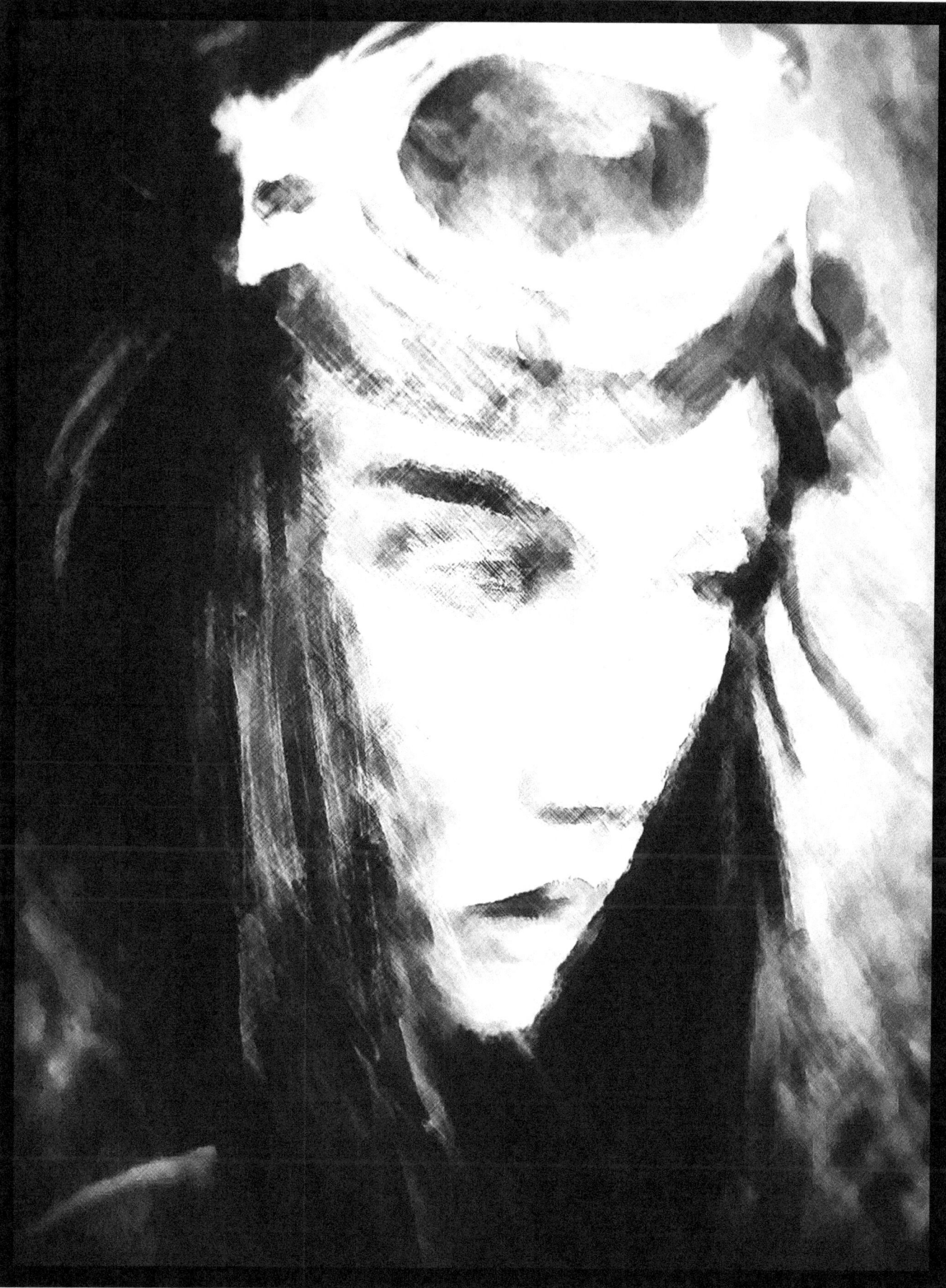

Copyright 2020 Clint Atelier Books
Auther&Artest: Clint Smith
ClintAtelier.com

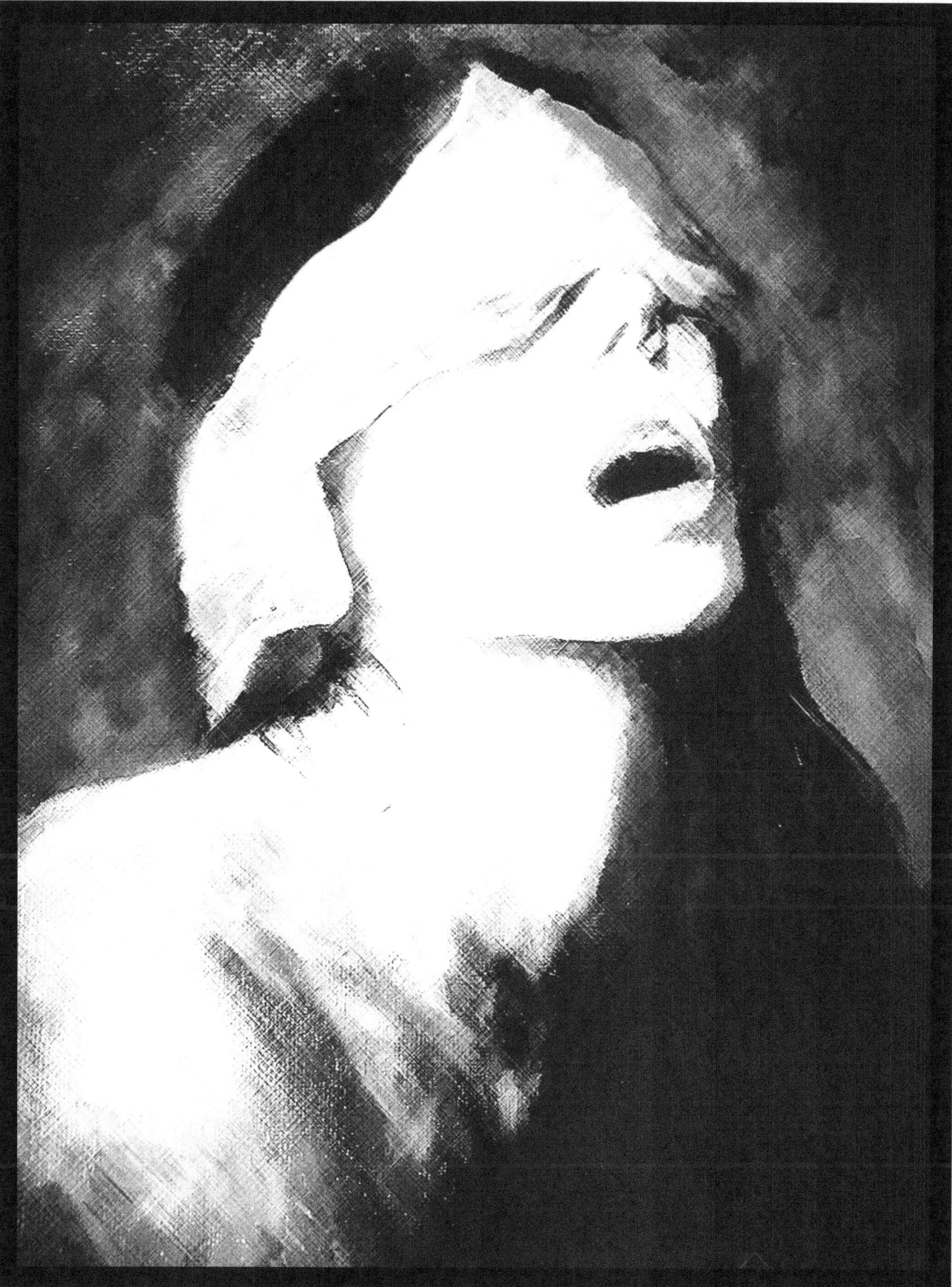

Copyright 2020 Clint Atelier Books
Auther&Artest: Clint Smith
ClintAtelier.com

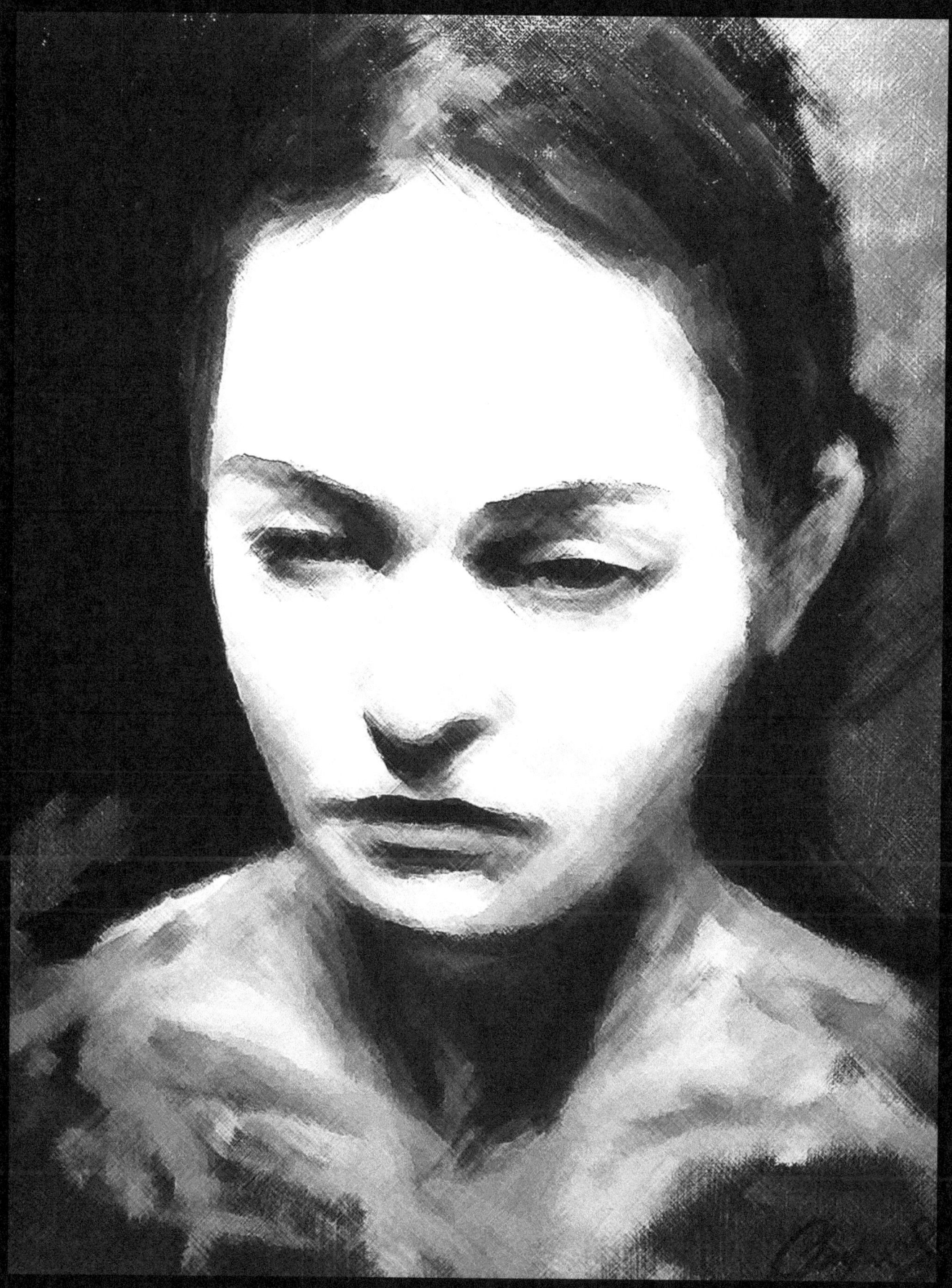

Copyright 2020 Clint Atelier Books
Auther&Artest: Clint Smith
ClintAtelier.com

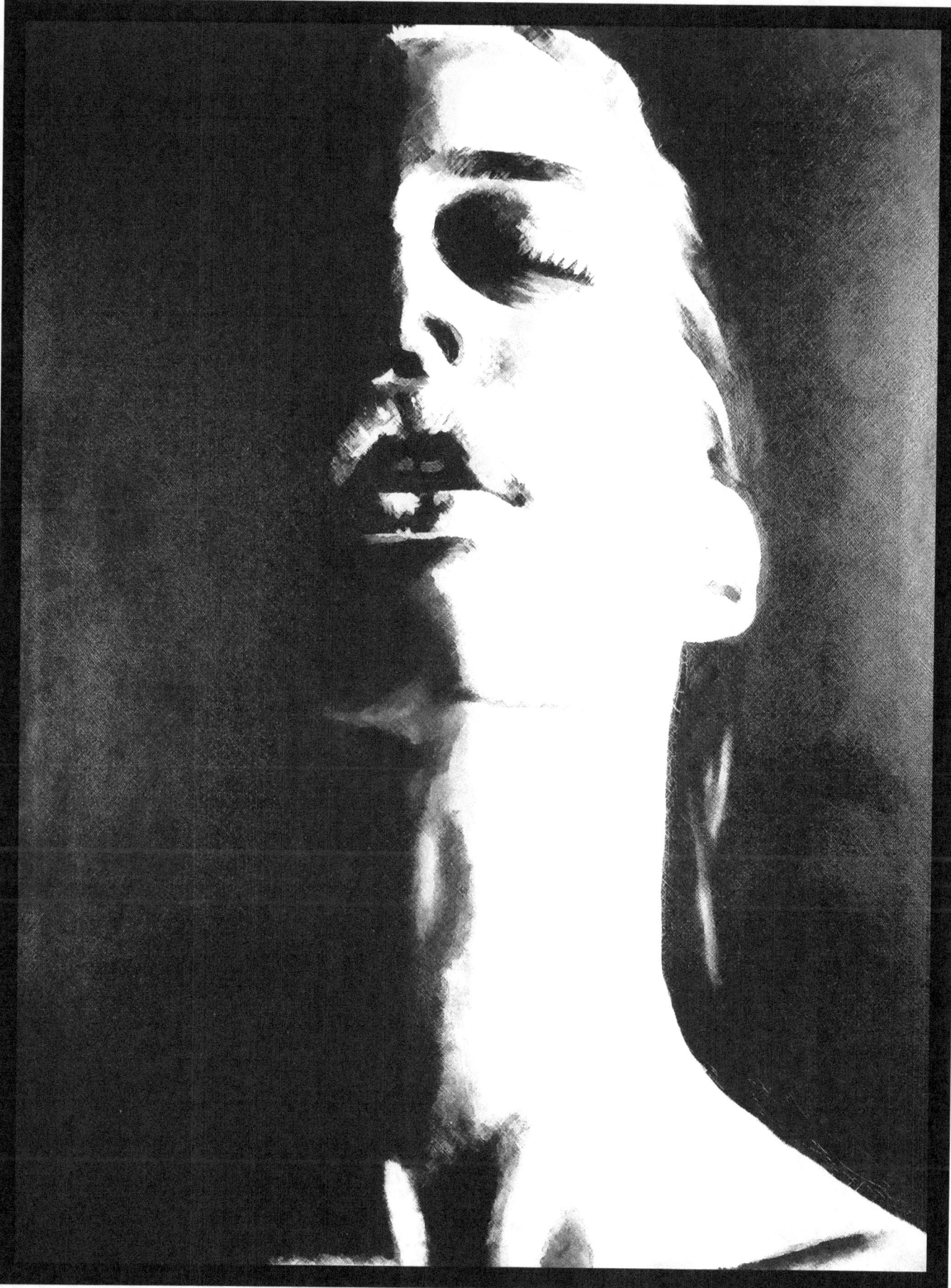

Copyright 2020 Clint Atelier Books
Auther&Artest: Clint Smith
ClintAtelier.com

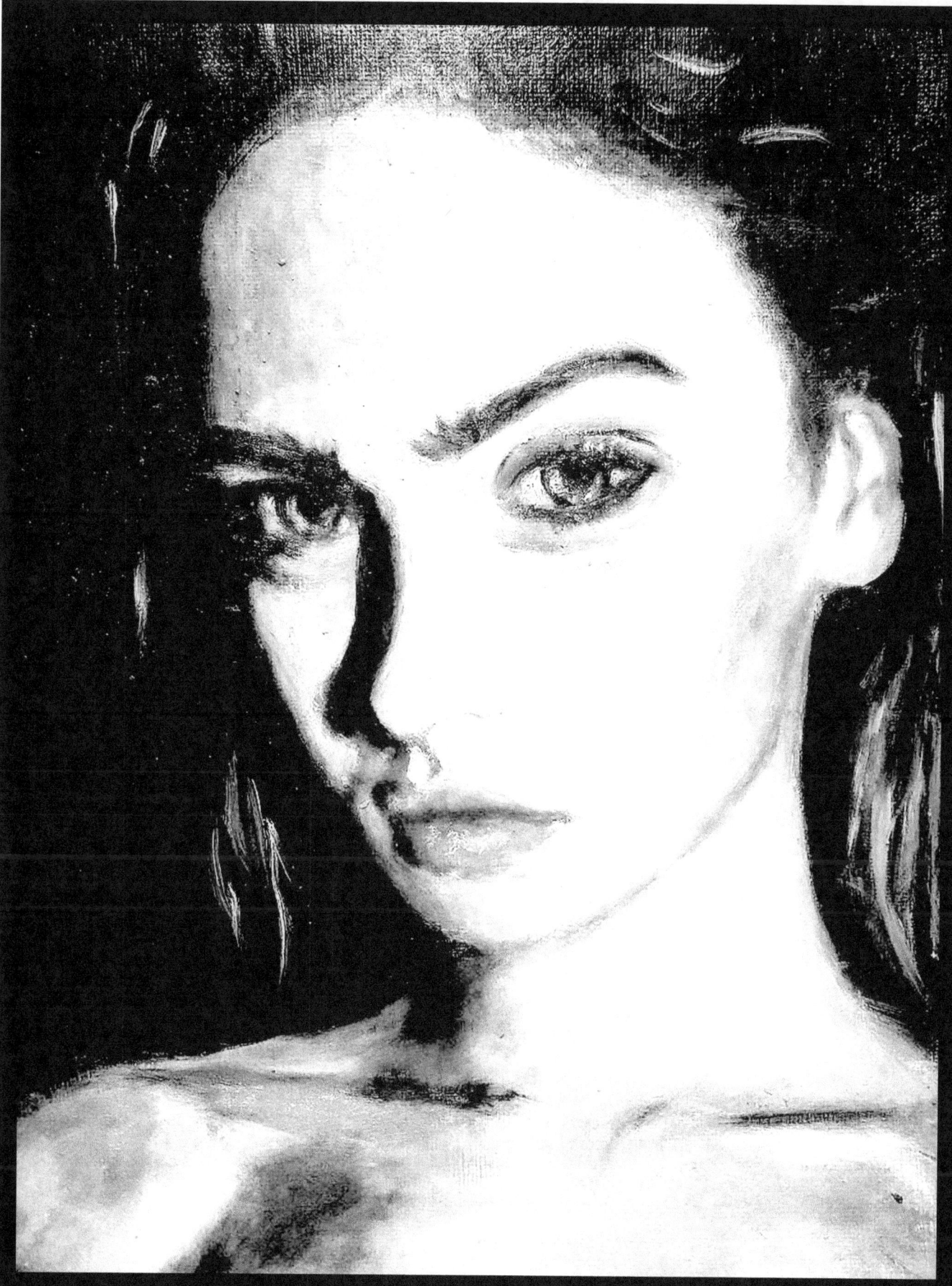

Copyright 2020 Clint Atelier Books
Auther&Artest: Clint Smith
ClintAtelier.com

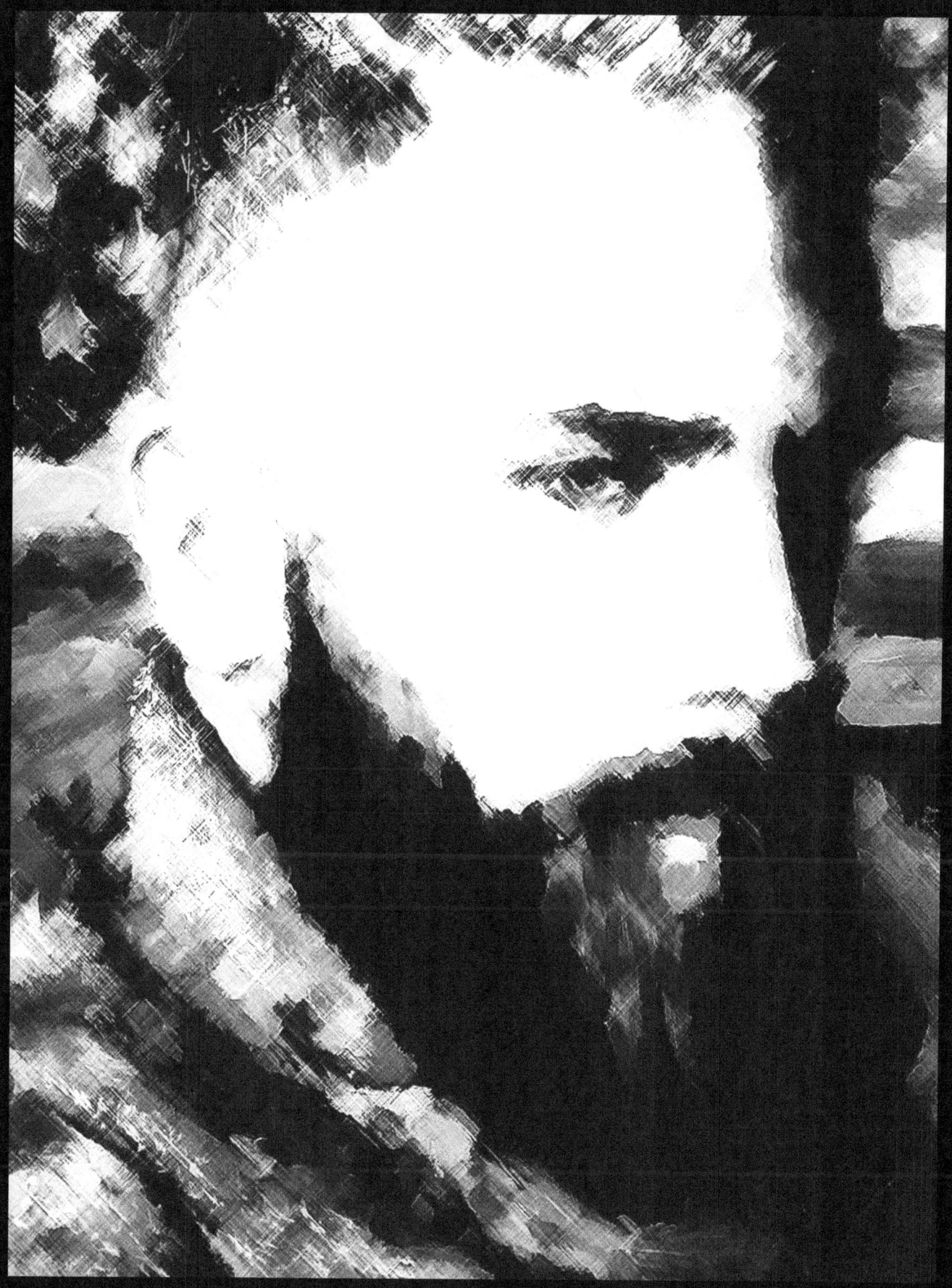

Copyright 2020 Clint Atelier Books
Auther&Artest: Clint Smith
ClintAtelier.com

www.ingramcontent.com/pod-product-compliance
Lightning Source LLC
Chambersburg PA
CBHW082020230526
45466CB00022B/2810